HOW DO YOU LIFT A LION?

Robert E. Wells

Albert Whitman & Company
Chicago, Illinois

Also by Robert E. Wells

Can We Share the World with Tigers?
Can You Count to a Googol?
Did a Dinosaur Drink This Water?
How Do You Know What Time It Is?
How Do You Lift a Lion?
Is a Blue Whale the Biggest Thing There Is?
Polar Bear, Why Is Your World Melting?
What's Faster Than a Speeding Cheetah?
What's Older Than a Giant Tortoise?
What's So Special about Planet Earth?
Why Do Elephants Need the Sun?

Library of Congress Cataloging-in-Publication Data

Wells, Robert E.
How do you lift a lion? / Robert E. Wells
p. cm.
1. Simple machines—Juvenile literature. 2. Machinery—Juvenile literature. [1. Simple machines. 2. Machinery.] 1. Title
TJ147.W44   1996   95-38323   621.8'11—dc20   CIP   AC

Text and illustrations copyright © 1996 by Robert E. Wells
Published in 1996 by Albert Whitman & Company
ISBN 978-0-8075-3421-2

Printed in China
27 26 25 24 23 NP 20 19 18 17 16

The illustration media are pen and acrylic.
Design by Susan B. Cohen

For more information about Albert Whitman & Company,
visit our web site at www.albertwhitman.com.

DID YOU EVER TRY TO LIFT A LION?

You'd have to be awfully strong.

It's because of the force of GRAVITY.

Gravity pulls objects downward.

When that object is as massive as a lion, it pulls pretty hard.

With a **LEVER**, you can lift a heavy weight with much less effort.

LOAD
SIDE

FULCRUM

FORCE SIDE

The main part of
a lever is a bar or
rod which balances,
or pivots, on
a FULCRUM.

If the **FORCE** side is longer than the **LOAD** side, you will have **LEVERAGE**.

Leverage adds force to your own strength.

With a force side this long, you could lift a lion!

Now do you suppose

LOAD
SIDE

FULCRUM

FORCE SIDE

The longer the force side is compared to the load side, the more leverage you will have.

So, if you had a lever
with a handle THIS long,

maybe you could
lift them a little!

Gravity is pulling down on that panda.

And there's also **FRICTION**
between the ground and the pallet.

Friction, or resistance,
happens when two surfaces
rub together.

The more weight
pushing on the
surfaces, the more
friction there is.

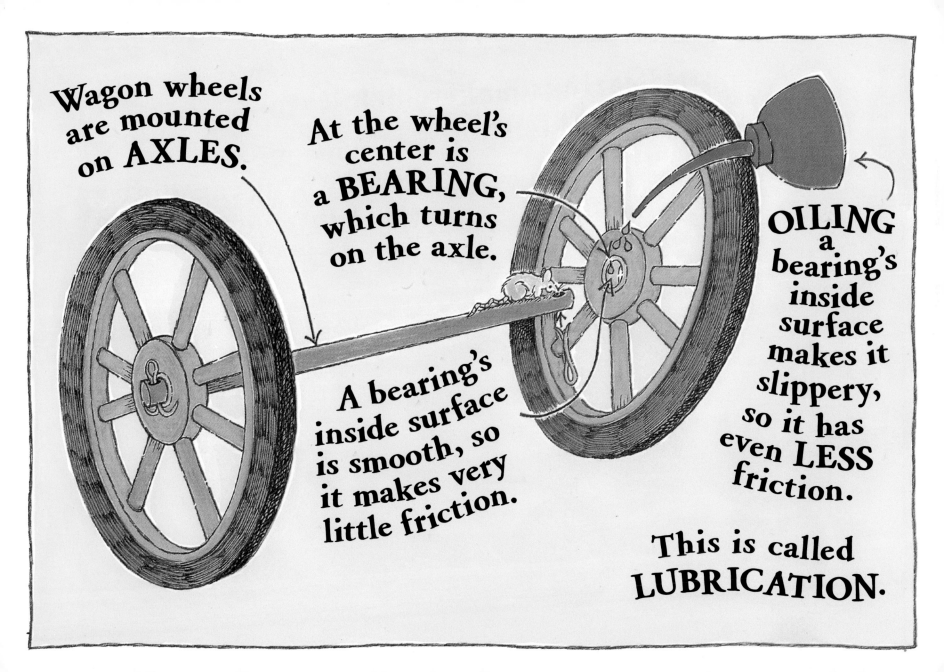

If you begin to go downhill, gravity takes over to pull your load.

Gravity not only pulls objects **STRAIGHT** down, it pulls them down slopes.

So now that you don't have to pull, you could carry a much **BIGGER** load!

PULL OF GRAVITY

DIRECTION OF OBJECT BEING PULLED BY GRAVITY

If the slope began to get VERY steep, you'd probably wish you had MORE friction to slow you down!

DID YOU
EVER TRY
TO DELIVER
A BIG BASKET
OF BANANAS
TO A BABOON
BIRTHDAY
PARTY?

It would be
mighty heavy.

With PULLEYS, it would be much easier to lift!

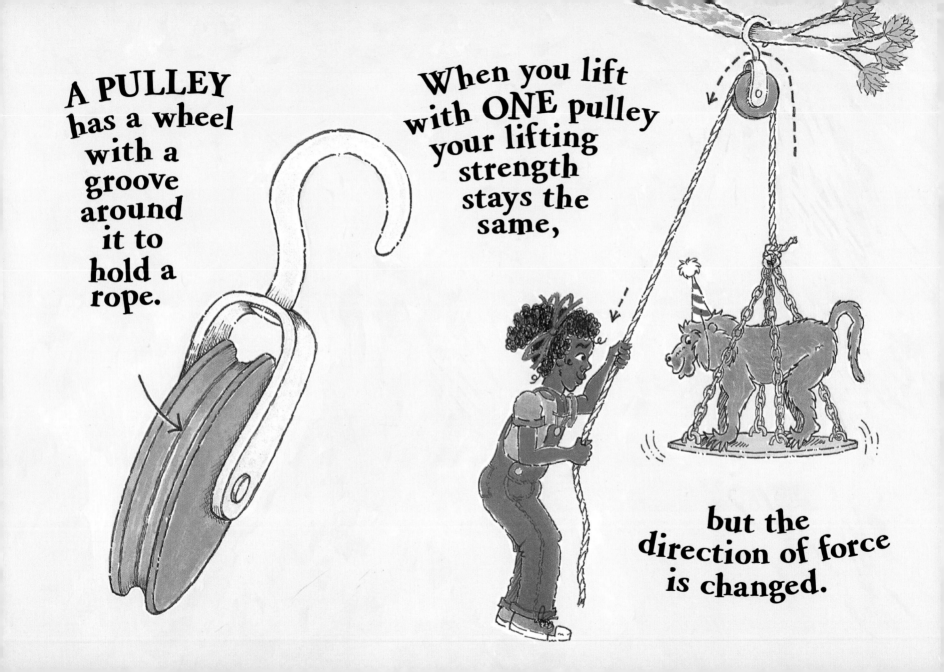

A PULLEY has a wheel with a groove around it to hold a rope.

When you lift with **ONE** pulley your lifting strength stays the same,

but the direction of force is changed.

Yes, pulleys make it
much easier to deliver
a big basket of
bananas to a baboon
birthday party,

but perhaps a SMALLER basket would have been better!

Our World Is Full of Simple Machines

The levers, wheels, and pulleys in this book are shown in just one of their many forms. Each of these simple machines comes in many sizes and shapes and can be used for many purposes. Yes, there are levers, wheels, and pulleys almost everywhere you look!

Did you know that when you row a boat, the oars are actually levers? Likewise, a screwdriver is a lever when you use it to pry the lid off a paint can. And when you cut a piece of paper, your scissors are two levers working together.

What would our lives be like without wheels? You'll find little ones on your skateboard, bigger ones on your bicycle, huge heavy ones on a train engine, and tiny ones inside some watches. There are other forms of wheels you might not even recognize, like the doorknob you turn to open your door or the faucet that turns off your water.

Pulleys pull you up in elevators and ski lifts. They help raise sails on sailboats and flags up flagpoles. With pulleys, a window-washer can lift himself or herself right up the side of a skyscraper.

Look around your world and you'll discover many more examples of levers, wheels, and pulleys.

How many can you identify?

Glossary

axle the supporting bar or rod on which a wheel turns. Sometimes an axle will support one wheel, as on a wheelbarrow; or two, as on a wagon.

bearing the part of the wheel which touches the axle as a wheel turns. There are three kinds of wheel bearings: sleeve bearings, roller bearings, and ball bearings. Sleeve bearings, the simplest kind, are shown in this book.

fulcrum the point on a lever which divides the force and load sides. When a lever moves, it pivots (turns) on the fulcrum, causing one side to go up and the other down.

leverage the increase in force or mechanical advantage that a lever provides. If a lever has a force side ten times as long as its load side, force is increased ten times—but the load side will move only one-tenth the distance.

lubrication a slippery substance, such as oil, applied to a surface. Lubrication reduces friction, so it helps parts move more smoothly. It also keeps them from getting too hot, since friction creates heat.

pulley a lifting device which uses a wheel with a groove around it to hold a rope. When two pulleys are used, as in the banana basket lifter, the load is supported by two sections of rope, each holding half the weight of the basket. Therefore, as the kids pull one section of rope, they are only lifting half the weight of the basket, but using twice as much rope.

simple machine the basic element of a complex machine. It does not have the many parts that complex machines have, such as ball bearings, gauges, gears, and valves. The lever, wheel, and pulley are all simple machines.